WHY SHOULD I EAT THIS?

HEALTHY FATS

TABLE OF CONTENTS

Healthy Fats 3

Glossary 22

Index 24

By Lindsay Snea

A Crabtree Seedlings Book

Crabtree Publishing

crabtreebooks.com

School-to-Home Support for Caregivers and Teachers

This book helps children grow by letting them practice reading. Here are a few guiding questions to help the reader with building his or her comprehension skills. Possible answers appear here in red.

Before Reading:

- What do I think this book is about?
    - *I think this book is about food.*
    - *I think this book is about healthy fats.*
- What do I want to learn about healthy fats?
    - *I want to learn which fats are the healthiest fats.*
    - *I want to learn what foods have healthy fats.*

During Reading:

- I wonder why...
    - *I wonder why eating fats keeps us fuller for longer.*
      I wonder why our bodies only need a little saturated fat.
- What have I learned so far?
    - *I have learned that eating fats gives us energy.*
    - *I have learned that eating the right kind of fat is important.*

After Reading:

- What details did I learn about healthy fats?
    - *I have learned that unsaturated fats are the healthiest fats to eat.*
    - *I have learned that healthy fats are an important part of our daily meals.*
- Read the book again and look for the glossary words.
    - *I see the word **vitamins** on page 3, and the word **energy** on page 4. The other glossary words are found on pages 22 and 23.*

HEALTHY FATS

Fat is a **nutrient** found in food. Healthy fats help your brain and body grow. They also help your body use important **vitamins**.

Eating fats helps you feel fuller longer and gives you **energy** throughout the day.

DID YOU KNOW?

Your body needs energy to play, to learn, and to grow.

Eating the right kind
of fat is important.

Different foods contain unsaturated, saturated, and trans fats.

Unsaturated fats are the healthiest fats. They are in foods such as nuts and seeds, salmon and tuna, and avocados, olives, and olive oil.

Saturated fats are in foods such as cheese, red meat, coconut oil, and butter. Your body only needs a little saturated fat.

Trans fats are unhealthy fats found in **processed** foods. These are foods that have been changed from their natural form, such as baked goods, frozen foods, and fried foods.

Eating too much saturated and trans fats can be bad for your health. It is important to choose foods with unsaturated fats whenever you can.

DID YOU KNOW?

Too much saturated and trans fats can be bad for your heart and make you sick over time.

Get in the habit of making good snack choices. Choose almonds instead of a muffin or cookies. Instead of bologna, snack on some cheese or Greek yogurt.

There are many ways to make healthy fats part of your daily meals. Good meals include toast with avocado for breakfast, a peanut butter sandwich for lunch, and salmon for dinner.

Making healthy fats a part of your daily diet will help protect your heart and brain all your life.

Glossary

energy (EN-er-jee): Your body or mind's ability to be active or do work

nutrient (NOO-tree-uhnt): A substance that your body needs to live and grow

processed (PROS-esd): Describing any food that has been changed from its natural form

vitamins (VAHY-tuh-mins): Nutrients found in foods that help your body grow and stay healthy

Index

brain 3, 20

daily diet 20

energy 4-5

nutrient 3

vitamins 3

About the Author

Lindsay Snea lives in the mountains of Fernie, British Columbia, Canada, with her husband and four children. Lindsay is an elementary school teacher, and a lifelong learner, who is passionate about cooking, food, fitness, being outdoors, and health.

Written by: Lindsay Snea
Designed by: Margaret Salter
Proofreader: Melissa Boyce
Photographs: All images from Shutterstock
Production manager: Candice Campbell

Crabtree Publishing

crabtreebooks.com 800-387-7650

In Canada: We acknowledge the financial support of the Government of Canada through the Canada Book Fund for our publishing activities.

Printed in the U.S.A./CP112025

Published in Canada
Crabtree Publishing
616 Welland Avenue
St. Catharines, Ontario
L2M 5V6

Published in the United States
Crabtree Publishing
347 Fifth Avenue
Suite 1402-145
New York, New York, 10016

Library and Archives Canada Cataloguing in Publication
Available at Library and Archives Canada

Library of Congress Cataloging-in-Publication Data
Available at the Library of Congress

Hardcover: 978-1-0398-8120-4
Paperback: 978-1-0398-8481-6
Ebook (pdf): 978-1-0398-8240-9
Epub: 978-1-0398-8360-4
Read-Along: 978-1-0398-8565-3
Audio: 978-1-0398-8523-3